EMMANUEL JOSEPH

Righteous Resolutions, Aligning Faith, Love, Career, and Ethical Business Practices

Copyright © 2025 by Emmanuel Joseph

All rights reserved. No part of this publication may be reproduced, stored or transmitted in any form or by any means, electronic, mechanical, photocopying, recording, scanning, or otherwise without written permission from the publisher. It is illegal to copy this book, post it to a website, or distribute it by any other means without permission.

First edition

This book was professionally typeset on Reedsy. Find out more at reedsy.com

Contents

1	Chapter 1	1
2	Chapter 1: The Power of Faith	3
3	Chapter 2: Love as a Guiding Principle	5
4	Chapter 3: Career as a Calling	7
5	Chapter 4: Ethical Business Practices	9
6	Chapter 5: Integrating Faith in Daily Life	11
7	Chapter 6: The Power of Commitment	13
8	Chapter 7: Balancing Love and Career	15
9	Chapter 8: Ethical Leadership: Leading with Integrity	17
10	Chapter 9: Faith and Love in Action	19
11	Chapter 10: The Intersection of Faith, Career, and Ethics	21
12	Chapter 11: Overcoming Challenges and Staying Resilient	23
13	Chapter 12: Crafting Your Own Righteous Resolutions	25

1

Chapter 1

Introduction

In a world that often feels fragmented and driven by conflicting priorities, the quest for balance and alignment in our lives becomes paramount. "Righteous Resolutions: Aligning Faith, Love, Career, and Ethical Business Practices" is a guide for those seeking a harmonious integration of their spiritual beliefs, personal relationships, professional aspirations, and ethical commitments. This book serves as a roadmap for navigating the complexities of modern life while staying true to one's core values.

Our journey begins with the exploration of faith, the cornerstone upon which a life of purpose and integrity is built. Faith, whether rooted in religion, spirituality, or personal conviction, provides a moral compass that guides our actions and decisions. It is a source of strength and resilience, helping us to weather life's storms and remain anchored in our principles.

From faith, we move to the transformative power of love. Love is the force that connects us to others and brings meaning and fulfillment to our lives. It encompasses self-love, romantic love, familial love, and altruistic love, each playing a vital role in our overall well-being. By embracing love as a guiding principle, we cultivate compassion, empathy, and a deep sense of connection with those around us.

The journey continues with an exploration of career as a calling. Work is not merely a means to an end; it is an opportunity to pursue our passions and make a meaningful impact. By aligning our career choices with our values and aspirations, we find greater satisfaction and purpose in our professional endeavors. Ethical business practices further enhance this alignment, ensuring that our work contributes positively to society and the environment.

Throughout the book, we emphasize the importance of commitment, resilience, and continuous growth. These qualities enable us to stay true to our resolutions, overcome challenges, and adapt to changing circumstances. By integrating faith, love, career, and ethics, we create a life that is not only successful but also deeply fulfilling and aligned with our highest ideals.

"Righteous Resolutions" is more than just a collection of principles and strategies; it is an invitation to embark on a transformative journey. It calls us to reflect on our values, set meaningful goals, and take actionable steps towards living a life of purpose and integrity. As you read through these pages, may you find inspiration, guidance, and the encouragement needed to craft your own righteous resolutions and create a life that truly resonates with your deepest convictions.

2

Chapter 1: The Power of Faith

Faith is the bedrock upon which our lives can be built, providing a strong foundation for our values, decisions, and actions. It is more than just a set of beliefs; it's a guiding force that shapes our moral compass and gives us the strength to navigate life's challenges. Whether rooted in religion, spirituality, or personal conviction, faith helps us remain resilient and hopeful, even in the face of adversity.

For many, faith provides a sense of purpose and meaning that transcends the material world. It encourages us to look beyond our immediate circumstances and consider the bigger picture. This perspective can be particularly helpful in times of uncertainty, offering a sense of direction and grounding. Faith also fosters a sense of community and connection, bringing people together in shared belief and mutual support.

However, faith is not just about passive belief; it requires active engagement and practice. This might involve regular spiritual or religious activities, such as prayer, meditation, or attending services. It could also mean living out our values in everyday actions, demonstrating integrity, kindness, and compassion in all that we do. By integrating faith into our daily lives, we can cultivate a sense of peace and fulfillment that comes from aligning our actions with our deepest values.

Ultimately, faith is a powerful tool for personal growth and transformation. It can help us overcome obstacles, build resilience, and find joy and satisfaction in life. By grounding our lives in faith, we can create a strong foundation for our resolutions, enabling us to pursue our goals with confidence and purpose.

3

Chapter 2: Love as a Guiding Principle

Love is the most powerful force in the universe, capable of transforming lives and building bridges between individuals and communities. It is a fundamental human need that drives us to connect with others and build meaningful relationships. Love can take many forms, including self-love, romantic love, familial love, and altruistic love, each playing a vital role in our overall well-being.

Self-love is the foundation of all other forms of love. It involves recognizing our own worth, taking care of our physical and emotional needs, and setting healthy boundaries. When we practice self-love, we become more resilient, confident, and capable of forming healthy relationships with others. It also enables us to show up fully in our interactions, offering genuine care and support.

Romantic love is often celebrated as one of the most profound and exhilarating experiences. It can bring immense joy and fulfillment, but it also requires effort, communication, and commitment. Building a strong romantic relationship involves understanding and appreciating each other's needs, working through conflicts, and growing together. When approached with mutual respect and dedication, romantic love can be a source of immense personal growth and happiness.

Familial love is the bond that ties us to our family members, providing a sense of belonging and security. It is often characterized by unconditional support and loyalty, offering a reliable source of strength during difficult times. Maintaining strong family connections involves staying connected, showing appreciation, and offering assistance when needed. These bonds can provide a stable foundation for navigating life's challenges.

Altruistic love, or love for humanity, extends beyond our immediate circle to encompass all beings. It involves acts of kindness, compassion, and service, often with no expectation of return. By practicing altruistic love, we contribute to the greater good and create a ripple effect of positivity and change. This form of love encourages us to look beyond our own needs and work towards a more just and compassionate world.

4

Chapter 3: Career as a Calling

A career is more than just a means to earn a living; it is an opportunity to fulfill our passions and make a meaningful contribution to the world. When we view our work as a calling, we approach it with a sense of purpose and dedication that goes beyond financial gain. This perspective can lead to greater job satisfaction, personal growth, and overall well-being.

Finding a career that aligns with our values and passions requires self-reflection and exploration. It involves identifying our strengths, interests, and the impact we want to make in the world. This process can be challenging, but it is essential for creating a fulfilling and meaningful professional life. By aligning our career choices with our true selves, we can find joy and purpose in our work.

Once we have identified our calling, it is important to pursue it with commitment and perseverance. This might involve acquiring new skills, seeking out opportunities for growth, and staying motivated despite setbacks. Building a successful career takes time and effort, but the rewards of doing work that aligns with our values are immeasurable. It can bring a sense of accomplishment, fulfillment, and pride.

Moreover, a career as a calling encourages us to consider the broader impact of our work. It prompts us to think about how our actions and decisions affect others and the environment. By adopting an ethical approach to our professional life, we can contribute to positive change and make a difference in the world. This perspective not only enhances our own sense of purpose but also inspires others to strive for excellence and integrity in their work.

5

Chapter 4: Ethical Business Practices

In today's world, ethical business practices are not just a moral imperative; they are also a key driver of long-term success. Companies that prioritize transparency, accountability, and social responsibility are better positioned to build trust with stakeholders, attract top talent, and achieve sustainable growth. This chapter explores the principles of ethical conduct in business and offers practical guidance for implementing them.

Transparency is the cornerstone of ethical business practices. It involves being open and honest with all stakeholders, including employees, customers, investors, and the community. This means providing accurate information, communicating openly about challenges and successes, and being willing to answer questions and address concerns. Transparency fosters trust and credibility, which are essential for building strong and lasting relationships.

Accountability is another crucial aspect of ethical business practices. It means taking responsibility for our actions and decisions, acknowledging mistakes, and making amends when necessary. Accountability requires a commitment to high standards of conduct and a willingness to be held to those standards. By holding ourselves and others accountable, we create a culture of integrity and respect that permeates the entire organization.

Social responsibility involves considering the broader impact of our business activities on society and the environment. This includes making ethical choices in areas such as sourcing materials, treatment of employees, and environmental sustainability. Socially responsible companies strive to create positive outcomes for all stakeholders, including communities and the planet. By prioritizing social responsibility, businesses can contribute to the greater good while also enhancing their own reputation and success.

Implementing ethical business practices requires a concerted effort from all levels of the organization. It involves setting clear ethical standards, providing training and resources, and fostering a culture that values integrity and accountability. By embedding ethics into the fabric of the organization, businesses can create a strong foundation for sustainable success and positive impact.

6

Chapter 5: Integrating Faith in Daily Life

Faith is not just a belief system; it is a way of life. Integrating faith into our daily activities involves living out our values and principles in every aspect of our lives. This chapter offers practical strategies for incorporating faith into our work, relationships, and personal growth, helping us to live with authenticity and purpose.

One way to integrate faith into daily life is by making ethical decisions that reflect our values. This involves considering the moral implications of our actions and choosing to do what is right, even when it is difficult. By consistently making ethical choices, we demonstrate our commitment to our faith and set an example for others to follow. This approach can lead to greater personal integrity and trust in our relationships.

Another important aspect of living out our faith is nurturing our spiritual well-being. This might involve regular practices such as prayer, meditation, or reading sacred texts. These activities help us stay connected to our faith and provide a sense of grounding and peace. They also offer opportunities for reflection and growth, allowing us to deepen our understanding of our beliefs and their role in our lives.

Building strong, supportive relationships is also key to integrating faith into our daily lives. By fostering connections based on mutual respect, compassion, and understanding, we create a network of support that can help us navigate life's challenges. This might involve participating in faith-based communities, volunteering, or simply being there for friends and family. Strong relationships provide a sense of belonging and reinforce our commitment to our values.

Finally, integrating faith into daily life involves continually striving for personal growth and self-improvement. This means setting goals, seeking out opportunities for learning, and being open to feedback and change. By dedicating ourselves to ongoing growth, we can live more fully in alignment with our faith and make a positive impact on the world around us.

7

Chapter 6: The Power of Commitment

Commitment is the driving force behind achieving our goals and staying true to our values. It involves making a promise to ourselves and others and following through with determination and perseverance. This chapter explores the importance of commitment in various aspects of life, from personal development to relationships and career.

Making commitments requires a clear understanding of our values and priorities. It involves setting realistic and meaningful goals that align with our beliefs and aspirations. By identifying what truly matters to us, we can focus our efforts on achieving those objectives. This clarity of purpose provides motivation and direction, helping us to stay on track even when faced with challenges.

Keeping commitments involves dedication and hard work. It requires us to be consistent, disciplined, and resilient in the face of obstacles. This might mean putting in extra effort, making sacrifices, or seeking support when needed. By staying true to our commitments, we build trust and credibility with others and reinforce our own sense of integrity and self-worth.

Commitment is also essential for building and maintaining strong relationships. Whether in romantic partnerships, friendships, or family connections, being reliable and dependable is key to fostering trust and mutual respect. This involves being present, actively listening, and offering support when needed. By honoring our commitments to others, we demonstrate our care and commitment to their well-being.

In the professional realm, commitment is crucial for achieving success and making a meaningful impact. This involves setting career goals, pursuing opportunities for success and contributing positively to our organizations. It means showing up consistently, delivering quality work, and continuously seeking ways to improve and add value. By committing to our professional development, we can achieve our career goals and make a lasting impact in our chosen fields.

In essence, commitment is the backbone of personal and professional success. It requires clarity of purpose, dedication, and resilience. By honoring our commitments, we build a life of integrity, trust, and fulfillment. This chapter underscores the importance of commitment and provides strategies for making and keeping promises that align with our values and aspirations.

8

Chapter 7: Balancing Love and Career

Striking a balance between love and career can be challenging, but it is essential for overall well-being and fulfillment. This chapter explores strategies for managing the demands of both personal and professional life, helping individuals to thrive in both areas.

Effective time management is crucial for balancing love and career. This involves setting priorities, creating a schedule that accommodates both work and personal time, and being disciplined about sticking to it. By allocating time for our loved ones and ourselves, we can ensure that we nurture our relationships and personal well-being without compromising our professional commitments.

Setting boundaries is another important aspect of achieving balance. This means being clear about our limits and communicating them to others. It might involve saying no to additional work or setting aside specific times for personal activities. By establishing and respecting boundaries, we can prevent burnout and maintain a healthy work-life balance.

Communication and support are also key to managing love and career. This involves being open and honest with our partners, family members, and colleagues about our needs and challenges. Seeking and offering support can help alleviate stress and create a collaborative environment. Building a strong support network can provide the encouragement and assistance needed to navigate the complexities of balancing personal and professional life.

Ultimately, balancing love and career is about making intentional choices and staying true to our values. It requires ongoing effort, flexibility, and a willingness to adapt as circumstances change. By prioritizing what matters most and being mindful of our time and energy, we can create a harmonious and fulfilling life that encompasses both love and career.

9

Chapter 8: Ethical Leadership: Leading with Integrity

Ethical leadership is essential for fostering a positive organizational culture and driving long-term success. This chapter examines the qualities of ethical leaders and their impact on teams and organizations, offering insights into leading with integrity.

An ethical leader is characterized by a strong sense of integrity and a commitment to doing what is right, even when it is difficult. This involves being honest, transparent, and accountable in all actions and decisions. Ethical leaders set an example for others to follow, creating a culture of trust and respect within the organization.

Empathy is another key quality of ethical leaders. This involves understanding and considering the perspectives and needs of others, and making decisions that are fair and compassionate. Ethical leaders prioritize the well-being of their team members and foster an inclusive and supportive environment. By showing empathy, leaders can build strong, collaborative relationships and enhance team morale.

Ethical leaders also demonstrate a commitment to social responsibility. This means considering the broader impact of their actions on society and the environment and striving to make positive contributions. Ethical leaders promote sustainability, diversity, and community engagement, setting a standard for corporate responsibility. By aligning organizational goals with ethical values, leaders can create a positive impact that extends beyond the company.

Leading with integrity requires a commitment to continuous learning and growth. Ethical leaders seek feedback, reflect on their actions, and strive to improve their leadership skills. They are open to new ideas and willing to adapt to changing circumstances. By fostering a culture of learning and innovation, ethical leaders can drive positive change and achieve long-term success.

10

Chapter 9: Faith and Love in Action

Faith and love are powerful forces for positive change in the world. This chapter highlights inspiring stories of individuals and communities who have translated their beliefs and compassion into impactful actions, demonstrating the transformative power of faith and love.

One example is the story of a community that came together to support a local family in need. Driven by their faith and love for their neighbors, individuals organized fundraisers, provided meals, and offered emotional support. Their collective efforts made a significant difference in the lives of the family and strengthened the bonds within the community. This story illustrates how faith and love can inspire acts of kindness and solidarity that have a lasting impact.

Another example is the work of an organization that promotes social justice and equality. Guided by their faith and commitment to love and compassion, the organization advocates for marginalized communities, provides resources and support, and works to create systemic change. Their efforts have led to tangible improvements in the lives of many and have inspired others to join the cause. This example shows how faith and love can drive meaningful social change and address pressing issues.

Faith-based and love-driven initiatives also play a crucial role in addressing global challenges. For instance, humanitarian organizations that provide aid and support to those affected by natural disasters, conflicts, or poverty are often motivated by a sense of faith and compassion. Their work not only alleviates suffering but also fosters hope and resilience in affected communities. These initiatives demonstrate the profound impact of faith and love in action.

Practical suggestions for getting involved and making a difference include volunteering, supporting charitable organizations, and advocating for causes we believe in. By taking action guided by faith and love, we can contribute to a better world and inspire others to do the same. This chapter encourages readers to translate their beliefs into positive actions that have a meaningful impact.

11

Chapter 10: The Intersection of Faith, Career, and Ethics

This chapter explores the intersection of faith, career, and ethics, illustrating how they influence and reinforce one another. By aligning our professional endeavors with our personal values and ethical standards, we can create a fulfilling and meaningful life.

Faith provides a moral compass that guides our actions and decisions in the workplace. It encourages us to act with integrity, treat others with respect, and strive for excellence in all that we do. By integrating faith into our professional lives, we can create a work environment that reflects our values and fosters a sense of purpose and fulfillment.

Ethics are the principles that define what is right and wrong in our professional conduct. They provide a framework for making decisions and taking actions that are fair, honest, and responsible. By adhering to ethical standards, we build trust and credibility with our colleagues, clients, and stakeholders. This commitment to ethics enhances our professional reputation and contributes to long-term success.

The alignment of faith and career involves finding work that resonates with our values and passions. This might mean choosing a profession that allows us to make a positive impact, pursuing opportunities for growth and development, and seeking out organizations that prioritize ethical conduct.

RIGHTEOUS RESOLUTIONS, ALIGNING FAITH, LOVE, CAREER, AND ETHICAL BUSINESS PRACTICES

By aligning our career with our faith and values, we can achieve greater job satisfaction and a sense of fulfillment.

Examples of individuals who have successfully integrated faith, career, and ethics in their lives offer valuable lessons and inspiration. These stories demonstrate that it is possible to achieve professional success while staying true to our values and making a positive impact on the world. By following their examples, we can navigate the complexities of our professional lives with integrity and purpose.

12

Chapter 11: Overcoming Challenges and Staying Resilient

Life is full of challenges, and staying true to our resolutions requires resilience. This chapter explores strategies for overcoming obstacles and maintaining faith, love, and ethical integrity in the face of adversity.

One of the key components of resilience is a positive mindset. This involves focusing on solutions rather than problems, maintaining hope and optimism, and believing in our ability to overcome challenges. A positive mindset can help us stay motivated and persistent, even when faced with setbacks. By cultivating a resilient attitude, we can navigate difficulties with greater ease and confidence.

Self-care is another important aspect of resilience. This involves taking care of our physical, emotional, and mental well-being. It might include activities such as exercise, meditation, spending time with loved ones, and pursuing hobbies and interests. By prioritizing self-care, we can recharge our energy and maintain the strength needed to face challenges.

Support networks play a crucial role in resilience. This includes family, friends, colleagues, and faith-based communities. Having a strong support system provides encouragement, advice, and assistance during difficult times. It also offers a sense of connection and belonging, which can be a source of strength and comfort. Building and maintaining these relationships is essential for staying resilient.

Finally, resilience involves a willingness to learn and grow from challenges. This means being open to feedback, reflecting on our experiences, and seeking opportunities for improvement. By embracing a growth mindset, we can turn obstacles into learning opportunities and emerge stronger and wiser. This chapter emphasizes the importance of resilience and offers practical strategies for staying true to our resolutions in the face of adversity.

13

Chapter 12: Crafting Your Own Righteous Resolutions

The final chapter provides a roadmap for readers to craft their own righteous resolutions. It offers practical advice on setting meaningful goals, creating action plans, and staying motivated to achieve them.

Setting meaningful goals involves identifying our core values and priorities. This means reflecting on what matters most to us and what we want to achieve in our personal and professional lives. By setting goals that align with our values, we can pursue them with greater passion and commitment.

Creating action plans involves breaking down our goals into smaller, manageable steps. This includes setting specific, measurable, achievable, relevant, and time-bound (SMART) objectives. By developing a clear action plan, we can stay focused and organized, making steady progress towards our goals.

Staying motivated requires ongoing effort and perseverance. This involves celebrating small victories, staying positive, and seeking support when needed. It also means being flexible and adapting our plans as circumstances change. By staying motivated, we can overcome obstacles and stay committed to our resolutions.

Exercises and reflection prompts in this chapter help readers identify their values, set goals, and create action plans. These tools provide a practical framework for crafting righteous resolutions that align faith, love, career, and ethical practices. By following this roadmap, readers can create a fulfilling life that aligns their faith, love, career, and ethical practices with their life's purpose.

Book Description

Righteous Resolutions: Aligning Faith, Love, Career, and Ethical Business Practices

In an ever-changing and often chaotic world, finding a sense of balance and alignment can be a challenging yet deeply rewarding pursuit. "Righteous Resolutions: Aligning Faith, Love, Career, and Ethical Business Practices" is a comprehensive guide that navigates this journey towards a harmonious life. This book is designed for those who seek to integrate their spiritual beliefs, personal relationships, professional aspirations, and ethical values into a cohesive and fulfilling existence.

The foundation of this book is built on four key pillars: faith, love, career, and ethics. Each chapter delves into these essential aspects of life, offering practical strategies, inspiring stories, and thoughtful reflections to help readers align their actions with their deepest values. Faith is explored as the guiding force that shapes our moral compass and provides a sense of purpose and resilience. Love is celebrated as the ultimate resolution that fosters meaningful connections and personal fulfillment.

The book also examines the concept of career as a calling, where passion meets purpose, and work becomes more than just a means to an end. It emphasizes the importance of pursuing professional endeavors that resonate with one's values and contribute positively to society. Ethical business practices are highlighted as the new standard for success, demonstrating how companies can thrive while upholding principles of transparency, accountability, and social responsibility.

Throughout "Righteous Resolutions," readers will find practical advice on setting meaningful goals, creating action plans, and staying motivated. The book provides tools and insights to overcome challenges, build resilience, and maintain a positive mindset. It also emphasizes the power of commitment

CHAPTER 12: CRAFTING YOUR OWN RIGHTEOUS RESOLUTIONS

and the importance of balancing personal and professional life.

Ultimately, this book is an invitation to embark on a transformative journey towards a life of purpose and integrity. It encourages readers to reflect on their values, craft their own righteous resolutions, and take actionable steps towards living a life that aligns with their highest ideals. "Righteous Resolutions: Aligning Faith, Love, Career, and Ethical Business Practices" is more than just a guide; it is a source of inspiration and empowerment for those seeking to create a meaningful and impactful life.

www.ingramcontent.com/pod-product-compliance
Lightning Source LLC
LaVergne TN
LVHW020742090526
838202LV00057BA/6186